SOLO CROSSING

SOLO CROSSING

Poems By

Meg Campbell

Paintings and Drawings By

Linda Bastian

July 19, 2000

For Catlin,

*With appreciation for years
of friendship — let's renew it
soon. So great to see you!*

love,

Meg

MIDMARCH ARTS PRESS
New York

www.solocrossing.com

Library of Congress Catalog Card Number 99-070238
ISBN 1-877675-31-8

Printed in the United States of America

Published in 1999 by
Midmarch Arts Press
300 Riverside Drive
New York, New York 10025

for Sara and Ken

Notes and Acknowledgements

I am grateful to the following journals where these poems first appeared:

Bellowing Ark, "Training Roses," "Swallowing Butterflies," and "Parting Instructions"

Caprice, "Court Date" and "On Breaking My Pelvis"

Medicinal Purposes, "4th Date: Walking on the Outside"

Moon Journal, "On Dancing with my Nieces, Ages One and Two and a Half"

Saturn: A New York City Periodical, "Ode to a Single Mother," "Night Dive," "Leave-taking," "Poems Sleep," and "I Never Wanted to Be a Poet"

Zip Lines, "To Take a Maple for a Lover"

"Heaven, Blow Through Me" first appeared in *Bedside Prayers* (HarperCollins, 1997)

"Airborne" first appeared in *Bless the Day* (Kodansha, 1998)

Special thanks to William Duke and Candace Wainwright for editorial assistance and encouragement and to my editor, Cynthia Navaretta, for guiding this work to publication.

Contents

Introduction

There is your truth, my truth and the truth.
     — Chinese Proverb

These poems are my truth from the past five years of my separation, divorce, and new life as a single woman and mother in mid-life.

My initial response to this trauma was to view it as an unexpected brain tumor: I would need a great deal of help and a willingness to try both new and familiar paths to healing. I turned to my faith, family, and friends as well as therapists, books, exercise, nature, and a divorce support group. If someone had suggested peach pits or homing pigeons, I would have followed instructions for both.

I wrote poetry in college, but had not written more than a half-dozen poems in the intervening nearly twenty years of marriage. When poems — at first, scraps and dream fragments — appeared in my journals, I was surprised. They became an insistent chorus demanding time and attention. My truth wanted out.

Succeeding in marriage was vitally important to me. I failed. I would have done anything to spare my children pain. I could not. Dating in my forties was not in my original life plan, nor was living alone with a vociferous cat.

Life surprises and teaches. I became a poet when I faced myself, excavated my interior, and brought the lantern I had long ago buried to the surface where it could shine.

These poems are my truth. May they help you find yours.

— *Meg Campbell*

WATCHING A GLACIER MELT IN JUNE

One summer vacation
father drove
hours out of our way
to Glacier National Park.
We rode a snowbomber
over fields of ice
not knowing where
the glacier began or ended.
The park ranger
said here — get out,
walk around.
These covered our continent.
Receding now.
I asked
"Can you see the glacier melt?"
expecting riverlets or brooks.

I couldn't see it melt that June.
Tonight sitting opposite you
on the back porch of my sister's house.
20 years ago, newlyweds,
we drove across the country. Carefree.
Now we are separated
eight months. You live
with another woman,
take her to your uncle's wedding,
tell me
you have an open heart
about us.
What heart?

I know thunderbolts
and lightning in my veins.
We see a counselor.
Agree to a summer of limbo
before a next step.
Divorce. Reconciliation.
We talk tonight at twilight.
The roses are in bloom.
These are facts,
debris embedded in an icy front.

I ask you
what your feelings are
about my feelings and
first you answer
with your thoughts.
I ask again
and then you
say
"I love you
I don't want to hurt you.
I want to hold you,
it makes me sad
when I see you cry."
And you cry saying these words
and I realize
I have been waiting since
I was 14
that summer
with my father
I've been waiting
to see a glacier melt
and maybe I never will.

WHEN REASON ALONE
WILL NOT SUFFICE

I look into your eyes,
feel coldness.
Ice gate closing
your heart from mine.
I give you reasons to let me in,
but reason alone will not suffice.
It was not reason
that erected fortress here.
Reason will not dismantle stone.
My hope then is to wait
and in the waiting time
befriend the sentinel.

At night in the distance
(but close, as waves in a conch shell)
I hear you singing a lullaby
as you sang to our first born.
By day, I make no sudden movements.
I listen. Sentry rarely speaks.
Sometimes at rest
he tells of damp caverns
where he grew up, alone.
Explaining it isn't cold here,
but familiar, home.

I bring a Japanese lantern one night,
poem the next.
A seashell. Rose petals.
Holly blue butterflies.
Eyelash from a wish.

Guard stares ahead.
When I have nothing more to bring,
I offer to sweep it all away
before I leave.

Turning, I feel his fingertips
upon my shoulder.
No, he whispers from deep within his chest.
Please stay.
I will take you to your love.
I turn to see the sentry flushed
and teary-eyed.
Your eyes of old. Anew.

There are no keys, the soldier says.
Each door opens
from the inside out.
A sparrow could push it free
but one must let within
one who will.
The man you love
sought refuge here as a boy.
Fireflies, hummingbirds
stir within the garden
of his soul.
He is afraid of light,
of hands reaching in
but they are not.
They seek sky.
Be patient yet.
He will find his way.
I shall miss his singing in the night.
Without him,
this castle stands an empty tomb.
May I come too?

SEPARATION

I.
Most set sail
across stormy seas
and never turn back.
In search of new lives
they try to leave
old wounds behind.
As if they could.
Their shipwrecked children
straggle to sand,
lost, whichever coast
they are washed upon.
Soul-weary at a tender age.

My hand is on the tiller
hugging shore.
Even now,
in this thick fog
when I can see
nothing,
hear nothing,
smell only ocean salt,
I hold lilacs
in my mind,
I hold you
in my heart.

II.
You said there was no passion.
You needed to be adored.
Then how you must adore her
to spin your life around her.
To give her all you treasure.
It was never adoration I sought or gave.
False worship to me.
I knew us both too well.

III.
I moor sailboat,
take down sails, alone.
I walk the path in dusk's filtered light
to an English cottage, built in 1842.
Our daughters are in the arbor
gathering roses, red and white.
They look up expectantly, clasping hands,
then turn away,
to see me latch gate shut.

IV.
Might moonlight dance upon cliffs?
Meet me there.
High above the roaring sea
away from sharks and rocks.
Come ashore.

I fan ember glow between us, still.

THE OTHER SIDE OF RAGE

Old rules don't apply.
Duck and roll.
Belly to the ground.
Wrapped in blanket.
having escaped burning blaze.
I got my daughters out
and went back in for me.

Building beyond repair,
collapsing
with one more footfall.
Firefighters at the window
clamoring on ladders
trying to pull me out.

What does it take?
What stops me?
Such sadness
I cannot feel flames,
scalding, skinning
ankles, cheeks, my palms.
I freeze.
Run! They shout.
No back door, no fire escape.
The only way out
through inferno of rage.
I want any other way.
Must I leap to death?
So I stay
crouched in sadness

and shame
in sadness
and tears
in sadness
and soundlessness
no voice.
Burning up.

Firefighters urge me on.
They race through fire
and know
I can survive.
Promise I will survive.
Voices strong, steady,
reaching me over and through
bellowing, crackling blaze
devouring my furniture,
my life,
my marriage,
myself as wife,
creating charcoal before my eyes.

I have to get out.

I scream.
It wasn't my fault.
You deceived me.
You lied to me.
I don't deserve this.
I am angry.
Angry! Angry!

Flames smack my face.
Legs race.
I scream
I pound.
Lungs rip out
to louder shrieks
shaking my groin
and far away
firefighters
scream too
angry
for what you have done to me.

My jaws unhinge.
I race forward
burn soles raw.
Screaming
with all life.

Like a tigress roaring.
running,
pounding,
roaring,
until
my singed and wounded paws
scratch window sill.
Rescuers pull me safe.
Bundle me in blanket,
carry me down twenty stories
rocking and holding me
until
I touch ground.

SOLO CROSSING

I cross the English channel
limbs coated with grease
reaching for France.
I cannot see
safety boat behind.

Swimming away
from old life.
Swimming towards
new life.
When I cannot lift my arm
another stroke
I understand
this is my life.
Swimming
alone.
Tired. Afraid.
How much longer can I last?

I reach again for shore.

MEETING HER BUTTERFLY

Broken-hearted woman
walking in the summer sun
watches blue butterfly
with deep orange spots
dance among columbine,
phlox, lady's slipper.
Indigo kimono, graceful arcs,
upstage the garden's path.
Butterfly alights
upon woman's index finger.
A kiss from God
whispering
"Stop. Listen. Listen."

ODE TO A SINGLE MOTHER

You never forget,
always scanning, tracking,
like a dog who dreams of running
and moves her legs in sleep.
You always run, awake —

MEDITATION AT DAWN

Inhaling blue angelfish
shimmering through pink coral.
Air sacs flutter,
cherry blossoms
opening and closing
with each wisp of breeze.
My daughter curls
in her dreaming sleep.
I am awake.
Breathing
deeper into ocean,
farther out to sea.

COURT DATE

It was our last date.
Sadness my mantle,
relief my veil.
Take the stand.
Tell the court
I agree my marriage
two decades, two children,
irretrievably broken down.
I remember fifteen years ago
the blue car broke down
and you left it.
Never went back.
How you puzzled me.
Or when you sobbed in my arms,
If you knew me, you would leave me.
I never knew.
When you walked
out
same age, same month
your father
walked
never looked back
I was bone certain
you would return.
Wake up from this nightmare.
You in love
with your masseuse.
Tell the court
the settlement
is just and fair.

I have not been coerced.
Judge leans forward
awaits my tear-streaked assent.
Clerk hands me water.
Voice unsteady
courtroom silence breaks.
Papers to sign
bend down
kiss top page.
Lipstick marking
goodbye
to myself
as a wife.

CARDINAL'S SONG IN SNOW

A red highlander beats drum
in winter branches overhead.
Tapping unseen piper
echoes back
amid falling baby's breath.
He waits, then swells his tufted chest.
Cascade of roses
I step forward, catch,
bow, then go.

MELANCHOLIA

When black dog appears,
welcome him home.
When he was a pup
I knew where his ears
liked to be scratched.
Nose nuzzled in my lap.
Black dog, back
from distant continents.
I lie with him watching fog roll in.
We cry in mist on the front porch swing.
I stroke his sleek, jet-black fur.
Paws rest upon my thighs
waiting for the moon to rise.

AURORA BOREALIS

When spirits
leave young flesh
they dance
with angels
who coax them from the mist,
greet them in warm sargasso sea
among iridescent bright blue angelfish
whose gills flutter like wings.
Angels spirit them to northern lights,
Sparkling there on coldest nights.
Hovering next to newborns
thrust early to earth
fighting for breath
amid cords, respirators,
fingers barely formed.
There, where angels rest,
spirits who leave young flesh
keep watch,
waiting their turn to cross,
to join a kindred soul
for life
or welcome home
returning light.

CONCRETION

In that ocean bed where you keep faith a secret,
a holy card lands next to your heart.
A petition to St. Jude
tucked years ago inside your wallet,
placed in the lined pocket
of your smart lawyer's suit.
Like sand chafing an oyster.
An irritant, a foreign object
mocks your briefcase, silk tie, shined shoes.
Claims dating twenty centuries back.
Latin and candles
and your grandfather
leaving Italy at sixteen.

You gently pry shell open,
praying,
lonely, longing for your pearl, your home,
holding luminosity in your palm
you marvel,
this is who you were, and are
and will become.

CLASSMATES IN
THE SCHOOL OF GRIEF

We are classmates in the school of grief.
Randomly assigned,
Rejected by lovers.
We loan each other pens,
Paper, prayer books.
Draw desks closer.
Whispering, laughing
Wandering back to younger selves.
Twinkly eyes.

We become toastmasters explaining
Feelings with precision.

Handsome you stand in cap and gown.
Your family, new girlfriend
Snap your photo admiringly.
I want to write in your yearbook
but words falter.
My daughters pull me by the hand —
Come, let's go.
Farewell, grief.

HEEDING ICARUS

Heaven must be blue
Baby blue, sky blue bands.
Tissue paper fading lighter,
darker.
Clouds cut out silhouettes.
A Western town's facade.
We do not go in,
but fly beside
on a par with clouds.
Playful, cherubic, billowy, puffy
wisps of cotton balls.
Then ahead Michelango's
snowy peaks,
daunting.
Turbulence,
the captain warns,
finding the right altitude.
We are not aboard a helicopter
or hummingbird that can suspend itself.
We press forward.
Tucking clouds into my mind
as we rush past.
Stately clouds. Starched.
Cloud cover stretches smooth
to the horizon, die-cut definition,
where I step into blue.

MORNING GLORIES

Morning glories dream two ways:
They catch their breaths,
pull corsets taut, curling skirts
over their hems.
Or they pleat sails —
stretched between star's five-point rigging —
around a mast.
Petals translucent holly blue,
luminous violet, musk rose.
Unfurled, they sing acapella
lips wide open hosannas.

Ariel artists, alpine climbers,
morning glories traverse trellis, arbor,
any picket or wispy string
to cast a spinneret upon.
Pioneer scouts pull the rest.
Siblings on the same shoot,
different hues,
share a common center —
snow banks,
sunshine deep in their throats.
When breezes kiss their cheeks,
they sway.

Sleepers by night,
morning glories proclaim
joy, day after day.
When autumn's cold seeps in
they hum.

Ballet dancers fluttering
at the farthest reach of stage
until color, music, life itself
takes leave.
Costumes from a Midsummer's Night Dream
strewn on a winter set.

GLADIOLUS

Generous in grief.
Dignified, erect
after mourners depart.
Accustomed to solitude
with the dead.
Plumed sentries to their passing.
Grateful for a different call.
As when I brought five home
set in water to sip, stretch.
Chrysalis dangling from stalks.
Strings of cocoons.
Milkweed pods burst,
white butterflies emerge.
Fluttery as organza dresses
at a Maypole dance,
ruffled christening caps.
Days they perch
until their balance lost.
Their wings fall
like medieval shroud.
My monkish duty
to lift cloth off the stand.
Attending their death
as they will one day mine.

DON'T POUR KEROSENE
ON THE ROSES

Don't pour kerosene on the roses.
Walk along the path.
Take flight to Rome, drive north,
friend guides me to a ledge.
He, Secretary of Interior,
zooms over precipice
in orange Citroen racing.
Straight shot down
shiny, slick, steep cliff.
I follow far behind,
grip steering wheel.
No footholds, tracks.
My car collapses
to a child's pedal cart,
my bare soles brake.
I jam them beating drums
to slow my speeding fall.
Alone and lost
my play car disappears,
and I slide into a grotto.
Friend motions me to join
as audience on stage
with six people singing opera.
Notes reverberate.
World's finest diva
delivers private aria,
no props, only a four-poster bed.
I nudge my guide bewildered.
"Listen," he says.
"Her words are English."
Don't pour kerosene on the roses.
Walk along the path.

PEONIES

Relief.
June starbursts
in magenta or white.
Ruffled crepe.
Peonies are scarce.
When present, abundant.

Roses rare kisses and jewels
in any garden.
Magnificent, majestic
on trellis, arbor or
basking in a sunny corner.

Next to elegant roses,
peonies are Parisian can-can girls
flouncing tissue petticoats.
Swaying into the wind.
Light on their stems.
Swirling dancers.
Side by side with roses
there is no competition.
Sisters never vie
for the same crown
if wisdom rules.

ONE LAST GRIEF TO MOURN

What shipwreck anniversary
has me by the throat?
Holds me dear,
lest I choke?
Wringing hands free
it is my limbs I must untwine
stumbling onto shore.
A splinter cast upon the sand,
seaweed tangled in my hair.
Still coughing, spitting
salt from out my lungs.
I pant and gasp.
To founder on this desolate shoal
again.

Final forgiveness
comes at last to free me
from the mire.
How did I not see?
Why discard warnings
given on the way?
And now these decades later
it is I, I must forgive,
for stepping through that fateful door,
aboard that ship destined to the reef.
To look upon myself stripped bare
as sure as rain must fall
I shed these tears for me.

4TH DATE:
WALKING ON THE OUTSIDE

You always
walk on the outside.
Water swirling clockwise down the drain,
as compass points north,
order from chaos
you walk on the outside.
Your grandmother
taught you well.

Horse-drawn carriages
splashing my silk taffeta?
Fending off marauders
scowling up 14th street?
You cover curbside.
An old custom
I am surprised
I notice,
surprised
I like.

You walk on the outside
as in waltzing
when the man
leads by pressing
his hand on the woman's back.
His palm whispering through her spine.
Gliding effortlessly
after dusk
before darkness

when sky is blue bunting
unfurled.
Worth pausing
to savor Bermuda sea
lapping tall buildings.
Then we walk again,
you on the outside.
Always.

NIGHT DIVE

Where paintings come from
Poems do too.
Reflected in your eyes —
the lake where you swim
late at night
alone in moonlight.
To wrest an image
you dive deep.
You go alone,
return to share
the painting that was always there
the poem yearning for breath and air.

ROPE SWING

A boy and a girl
linger at the rope swing.
Strong swimmers, timid jumpers.
They spend summers watching others leap.
They who never venture far
from muddy banks aloft,
yearn for wingspan, height.
One autumn dusk, alone
one paddles out
to throw the rope swing back.
Taking turns,
both false start.
Risk crashing branches,
solo nosedives.
Try and try again
until one yanks the other
holding tight.
Ascending
farthest, highest peak,
they let go
and tumble sweetly
into darkness
touching stars
within their reach.

BLUE NECTAR

If I show you the note card
taped to my journal
of two wooden-shuttered French doors
side by side, each blue,
with iron balconies and flower boxes
filled with pink and red geraniums,

Will you look closely,
will you stroke my cheek?
Ask me why do I love this photograph so?
Will you listen
as I search for words?
You furrow your brow,
say ever so gently —

Come now out with it.
And I tell you of blue —
blue butterflies, blue china plates,
cobalt blue gingham linens, indigo blue,
the blue of the Pacific, Mary Star of the Sea,
blue sky, your blue eyes,
how I am drawn to blue
as a bee to nectar.

RABBITS IN SNOW BURROW DEEP

Your goodbye began in silence,
snowflakes I would not hear.
Until my ears had frostbite,
cupping them no use.
I had to come in from the cold.
Rabbits in snow burrow deep.
I envy them their warmth,
shared breath.

WHAT I MISS

Nuzzling in the length of your arm
between your chest and the book of poems
open before us.
Celestial navigator, you scan stars,
voice earnest and frank.
A flawless, moonlit sail.
I miss the quick kiss you give
turning the page
and long slow ones you press
as you lay poetry aside,
shift my shoulders, torso, so we face.
Pausing between embraces,
as in the moment before a Japanese bow
when eyes deeply meet.
Our eyes open and shut
slowly, as if we reside underwater,
leave our coral reef for air
only when we must.

CROCUSES

Crocuses stake banners close to ground.
Humble, patient.
Persephone's periscopes.
Noah's doves on a mission.
Scattered Swiss dots.
When gathered in Shriner's convention,
velvet hats bold against March's drab carpet.
Brass bands.
Gospel choirs in dark purple robes.
Synchronized
as infant birds straining gullets,
beaks wide for sustenance.
Wine goblets filled on a sideboard
before guests arrive
to raise stems in toast.

THE TERMS OF SURRENDER

Despair harpoons me.
Drags me hard, fast on sharp hook.
Ripped from an airplane,
inhaled by wind.
Fighting its pull,
thrashing, bullfight panic
takes me farther out to sea.
Heading straight back
as I came,
I will drown.
I need stillness, wits
clearing beyond wits.
I drag myself there.
Stabbing water engulfs and yanks.
I unpeel my eyes from sand, pivot left,
crank arms, propel legs,
crawl ragged diagonal to shore.
A migrating bird caught in a hailstorm
who knows nothing
except this is the route to warmth.
A sentry crossing enemy lines before ceasefire,
dodging bullets.
The terms of surrender written in graceful longhand,
folded, pressed close to my heart.

PENNY WHISTLE WELCOME

Elevator jammed.
Corporate types.
A month since seeing you.
Few words
only goodbye.
Now evening out.
Not a date.
Friends.
How to greet you?
Will you kiss my cheek
or remain in clouds?
Doors open, crowded foyer.
Startled,
I hear toe-tapping music —
part bagpipe, reed.
See you standing
magic lantern in hands
releasing finches, canaries.
Pan in the 7th floor hallway.
Children pause, tug parents' hands.
Smiling, laughing,
I walk toward your
penny whistle welcome.
You take a breath —
wingtip glances my cheek —
then play again.
Anasazi flutist on a mesa
serenading sunset,
fife player on Emerald Isle
awakening dawn.

TRAINING ROSES

I train roses.
June's graduating class,
rowdy crowd in circus tent.
In top hat,
I call forth climbers.
Teach them stunts
so they dazzle at heights,
swinging trapeze or high wire.
I gather thorny clumps of branches
and stake them with twine
else their garlands droop.
Understudies never called.
Summer will be closed,
popcorn ground into sawdust
and children will ask,
"Did we sleep through the fireworks?"

I plead with creeping roses.
They must go on.
For the sake of middle-aged folk
who shake heads in disbelief
to awake at six a.m.
and rush to hoses
to give herds water.
As if roses were elephants.

Roses. I train them.
They prick back.
Their petals,
luscious red, white,

peach, pink, yellow —
proclaim another tale.
Rapunzel triumphant
in the tower.
Lions who roar.

I prune a branch here, there.
Bring a cutting indoors.
They pierce my dreams.
Fall through snow to my pillow.
Each one a vial
of ancient fragrance.
Alone in the big top
late this night
we rehearse one last time.
I put them to bed.
Think they are asleep.
When I check them at midnight
they are wide awake,
waving to friends in the breeze.

HEAVEN, BLOW THROUGH ME

Heaven, blow through me.
Lift me past edges of my life.
Cast me in a clearer light.
Scoop me up trembling, spent.
Certain I have nothing left to give.
Give me comfort, solace,
blood flowing through my heart.
That I breathe Your breath
at last.

GARDENIAS

Pesky creatures,
yanking at my elbow.
Please, a poem.
Attach us to a bush
beneath bedroom window,
Hot Springs, Arkansas.
Sweltering summer nights
when love seemed
birthright, possible.
Fragrance sweet, laden
as honey and ivory petals
silky, strong and
tucked behind a young bride's ear.
Years later,
alone in a city inhospitable
to gardenias, I hear them
pestering me to make them into
a corsage, or cut flowers
floating in water.
Savannah blossoms
from my old life.
Distant, foreign.
Gardenias plead with me
not to be left behind.

LAST POEM

If I knew
this were my last poem
would I stay at my desk
scratching ink on paper,
crossing out lines,
pausing, trying again?
Would I slam my journal shut,
crawl inside the poem?
Look at it from its point of view?
Lodged in brain tissue.
Strain to find translator,
passport, release.
Maybe we'll stay put.
Let blood rush by.
Peer through back side
of eyes. Stretch to scratch
inside cap of my skull.
Tickle chords to ears.
Stop chasing poems,
any poem, this poem.
Be still.
Come.

LEAVE-TAKING

I drive you to college today.
Daughter who made me mother,
resident of my flesh and mind
before birth, conception,
when I was in love
with idea of being your mother.
Then you barrelled out, squealing.
I fell through canyon walls
past granite demands
to mossy landing where you suckled.
Cuddled, called mommy, mommy
when lost or frightened.
Mommy, mommy from fevers,
nightmares. Shaking me from dreams.
Months you kicked within,
years worried
how you fared without.
Were you happy?
You climbed steep cliffs.
Stand now on continent's rim.
Leaving me.
Little one. Woman.
Go in peace.
Fly home when you can.

I NEVER WANTED TO BE A POET

I never wanted to be a poet.
Useless. Ignored. Marginal.
Vestigial. Anachronistic. Simpering.
Needy. Craving recognition.
An audience. Cymbals clanging.
Spoons on water glasses.
Lugging that magic wand with fairy dust
everywhere. To the past.
To dinner out.
Stoking dream life like a hot iron.
Never a moment's peace.
Who would chooose that?

ON MY FATHER HAVING
OPEN-HEART SURGERY

Again?
Slashed your chest open before.
Dug hands in,
wanted to still your heart.
Stop you from leaving.

Now, at 72, you call to say
you have open-heart surgery tomorrow.
I wish you well. Stunned
cannot summon more.
Reach deep, say "I love you."
Silence, then you say,
"I talked to four chaplains today."
Try to recall a time when you
said the words back, or first.

Graduating from high school,
you asked,
Why didn't you win any prizes?
Asked me not to have a wedding.
Begged you to see your granddaughters
dance in Nutcracker.
Busy working, still busy working.

We were six spaniel pups
panting for your approval.
You gave me a drawer in your desk.
Once left me a note
"Thanks for being."

Surprise gift of a telescope when ten.
Asked for climbing trees
when eleven.
Planted sycamore and maple
in southern California.
You promised they would grow.
Brought sprigs of night-blooming jasmine
to my pillow.
This you —
caught in glimpses,
goodness, understanding.
Hung onto like a pit bull
years after you'd gone.

To rip yourself from our lives,
felt like you were choosing death.
When strangers face each other
build from there.
Time against us.
Surgery at eight.
Ask you what I can do.
"Pray for me."

ST. TERESA'S ROSE GARDEN

Oddest thing. A novena.
To her? Pale waif?
Life spun out in a convent courtyard.
Merciless on herself.
She's the one?
Plaster statues in bathtubs on front lawns.
I'm going for her? Ms. Plain Jane.
"Send me a rose from your heavenly garden,"
I plead on my knees.

POEMS SLEEP

Poems sleep naked between pages of a book
until our eyes rest there.
Reading them, they quickly dress.
But cannot speak except through us.
We are their breath,
tether from their time to ours.
Old now, we missed them in their bloom,
but aged, character display.

Poems sleep as princess under spell
until we a prince become.
Mount horse,
beauty, truth, adventure seek.
All we need to know.
Must slowly pass through forest dense
to find a body dreaming there.
In haste, many have we missed.

But not today.
Gingerly dry leaves we tread.
In sunlit clearing see her there.
Her hair a cape on shoulders rests.
Bending with a kiss,
this is another poem being read.
Somewhere.
In woods. Lips meet.
She awakens, speaking now
voice clearer, richer
yet our own.
Loveliness in our embrace
through vessel of our hearts,
our minds, our mouths.

MEETING YOUR FATHER
ON PARK AVENUE

Fathers begin in footlights.
Daughters sit rapt in the front row.
Through act one betrayals
to love's triumph as the curtain falls.
Singing to a full house, to one.
Lullabies, Happy Birthday, Sunday hymns.

But your father really was a Broadway star.
We hear him sing
Oklahoma, Kismet, Kiss Me Kate.
You point out a long passage
where he doesn't pause for breath,
but sings on, words a wave's force
breaking on shore.
You want me to hear.
Tell me his ashes rest
in a handmade box
in a closet in your bedroom.
Three years, waiting for your mother
to take them to the cemetery.
She may never be ready.
He waits.

It is morning, sun streams onto your face.
Your head is tilted,
listening to your father sing.
He is on stage, in costume,
gesturing with his hands.
Voice resonates.

He lifts every care
matinees and evenings
until the run ends.
You go backstage
watch him scrub
his makeup off.
Have him to yourself,
again.

DANCING WITH MY NIECES, AGES ONE AND TWO AND A HALF

Parents out, house ours.
After baths, "Where shall we dance?"
Elder dashes to parents' room.
"Here. I can put the tape on
myself." Music loud.
Younger wobbles in place.
Hula dancer on dashboard.
Watches us cavort,
kick legs, sway, clap hands.
Tapping bones loose,
we are three saucers spinning.

Our Rumpelstiltskin frenzied jig
summons my daughters from memory.
Scampering in sleepers
across fifteen years.
Singing,
"We are the dancing girls."
Hold them in my arms.

Put straw hats on nieces.
Tiaras on princesses
whose slippers cannot stop.
Swooping cub up, hoist overhead.
She chortles, reaches for ceiling.
Elder clamors for turn.
"Little reindeer flying,"
torso flat on my outstretched arms.
"Big reindeer," she insists.

"Make me go upside down."
Fold her to a somersault on rug.
Tape clicks off.
She pokes her head through silence.
Alarmed music may end,
as it must.

BLUE HERONS

Alone on marshy shore
when heron lifts its wings from grass.
Lightness itself with air blue cast.
I looked for others across the marsh,
supple blades in dusk's faint breeze.
Watched them with their parson's gait.
Bowed, spindly, sheriff's swagger.
Heels first, long necks close behind.
Ridiculous on land,
but then in sky again to trees
or landing as on fontanelle.

Blue heron watch,
I keep it yet.
On train hope rustling paper
is sound of wings, sound of my heart
where once I came to grieve.
Blue herons live there still.

TURNING 10 AGAIN

This year
I'm turning 10 again.
In sun years, I'll be 45.
But really I'm cycling back to 10.

Fifth grade when Sr. Fidelia
assigned me to the back corner
in the middle of the four worst boys
who cursed around me.
I asked my mother
what does shit mean?
She told me to scoop up our dog's poop
and take it to school in a brown lunch bag
and next time Ricky Doyle said "shit"
to reach into my desk and say,
"Is this what you want?"
I couldn't do that.
Now he's dead, drowned fixing his sailboat.
I'm turning 10 again.
Fat then, I rode my bike after school
to the pillboxes at the end of the street,
panting uphill. Loving downhill coast home,
weightless, flying.
Now I'm riding my bike from Boston
to New York. People don't believe me.
They forget I'm turning 10.

AIRBORNE

My mother, 72,
turns to the handsome man seated beside
her on the plane.
"I bet you were hoping to sit next to
an attractive young blonde."
Smiling, he replies, "I am."

KITTY HAWK, NORTH CAROLINA

waking morning after
spouse's wedding.
crows en masse
rising from my chest.
He has a stroke now —
it's
her
problem.

SLEEP

Sleep comes upon me
as clover wild in a field
comes upon spring.
Or twenty singing finches
in the garage of my auto mechanic,
in a flurry.
Surprising even after frequent visits.
Not expecting dashes of brilliant yellow
darting in a room
with cars' underbellies exposed,
diesel in the air.
Standing at songbirds' cage,
gazing through mesh
I fly.

PARTING INSTRUCTIONS

Swallow clouds
as whales graze plankton.
Coast ocean fields, mouth wide.

Braid honeysuckle into your hair.
Wear peacocks' cast-off feathers.
Dress warmly.
High altitudes where you are going,
air has a nip.

Steamed milk with nutmeg, honey —
sip slowly.
Savor light and fluffy.
Let froth remind you.
And your fingertips kneading dough.

AFTER CANCER
for L. W.

My shoulder blade?
I tossed it to the sky.
Needing, wanting speed,
less weight.
Reached back, pulled arrow
from my quiver.
Aiming high,
it fell to shark-infested waters.
Now my body
a different constellation makes.
No missing stars, only a hollow
where my love
bestows flame.

AFTER THE STORM

My red maple's left branch
severed, downed.
Gardener removes hulk, bouquet.
Tree's marrow exposed to air.
Scalpel cuts clean, spare.
Watching wound heal, weeks pass.
Welcome first buds
in stalk that remains.
Half a canopy outstretched to sky.
Like when a parent dies.
Arm ripped from socket,
we stand. Fruit-bearing
yet missing reach to clouds.
Shade elder provides.

TRIGGERS

It is our night to finish our manuscript.
Sitting at the desk in your apartment
hearing you telephone your daughters from the next room,
I spell-check the poem I wrote about the last time
my husband told me "I love you."
His words drained of meaning, no relation to deed.
It was why later I wasn't looking for declarations
from you, back when we were —
we were, what? — I
was falling in love with you, but
never spoke the words because I feared
your cardiac arrest. Tonight,
in front of your computer screen,
mumbling a prayer for strength and grace,
I hear those words roll off your tongue
to your daughters, as is right. I know this,
but your words fly effortlessly as doves
released from captivity and I am filled with regret
that none ever alighted on my shoulder
back in that time when it might have been true.
Sad I lacked courage
to speak my heart.
Even now, startled,
I cannot corral words to past tense to share aloud,
report shard of Greek vase found in a ruin.
They stream into present,
magpies causing havoc I beat them back.
Then I hear you calling your girlfriend
to confirm your sailing date — just moments before
I scrolled through your poem about your marriage,

how you always sailed alone.
And I think how as your friend,
I ought to be happy
for your happiness.
But I pounce at you
when you walk into the room.
Scowling how rude you are
when what I'm feeling is
it hurts to be in this place so rich
in memories for me.
I'll try new places,
but earlier in your office at your new job,
watching you on the phone deftly persuading
a colleague to your point of view,
catching your glances — Atlantic blue eyes —
I savored you.
Let my heart gates open for a moment
in the pure pleasure of loving you.
See, it is a dove I offer
to the orchids in your heart.
Silent doves going I know not where.

TO TAKE A MAPLE FOR A LOVER

To take a maple for a lover
requires constancy.
Beloved lion on this pond shows age.
I'll dance with him tonight.
Below canopy, my forehead leans
upon his gnarled bark.
Lichen muted green I've seen upon the sea.
Our steps are slow — none to naked eye —
but we bring more than nakedness to this dance.
He offers golden fleece, peach rinsed.
Tangled branches veteran of winter storms.
I bring legs,
arms to hold him in my embrace.
He silent roots, sound of falling leaves.

THE WAY TO SURVIVE DIVORCE

The way to survive divorce
is with your hands.
Examine them. Speak to them.
Heed their reply.
Watch where they lead and follow.
To the garden. To the kiln.
To the tiller on high seas.

Didn't they teach you to walk?
Dress rehearsal on knees,
scouts scurrying ahead?

You married with your hands.
Ring finger all that.
Canada geese migrating south,
hands will lead you out.

Mine have. Pen held in palm.
My mother's did.
Playing piano.
She dragged them like lumps of clay
to the keyboard in grief.
Pressing keys, they grew light and supple.
Night after night she played Broadway hits
and sang.
Slipping out from the weight of her pain
to the piano bar at La Valencia
or onboard a cruise ship
where music swirls with gaiety.

It is her hands,
I see plainly tonight.
At seventy-three, her fingers dart across keys,
nimbly bringing arms along.
Shoulders lift with syncopated rhythm.
Seated at the piano bench,
feet tapping pedals and singing,
she is a passionate flamenco dancer
whirling castanets.
Unveiling her heart
with her hands.

OPEN HEART

Lift bluefish from pavement
back into my chest.
Slip it between slender bones.
Ribs protect, encase as coral,
yet with every breath
swell or constrict.
Living bones corset heart
too long in sun and shade
its color fades, needs rest.
Dark quiet save for pumping blood.
Steady drumming, pulsing
through my night. Lace close my tissue,
flesh shutters louvered as my skin
to let air in, filtered light. Whole I stride
the way a woman who
has reclaimed her heart.
Returned it to its cavity,
home. Ceding nothing
trading slashed chest, heart dangling
as a pear ripe ready to fall
for stitches, this:
heart safe within me
even as we speak.

INVITING MISS E. DICKINSON
TO GO DANCING

She puts up every excuse
and a final, firm no.
But I persist, standing in her foyer
and say, "Get your wrap.
We are going to the dance."
She fusses, nothing to wear,
but pats her bodice, adjusts shawl,
tugs at her waist.
Catches sight of her smile,
a wisp of candle smoke, in the hallway mirror.
"Even watching will be fun," I insist,
linking arms, skirts swishing
as we descend her stairs.

ON BREAKING MY PUBIC BONE AND RIBS WHEN MY BICYCLE SKIDDED ON GRAVEL

Sweet bird swooping on an upwind
crashing into a huge pane of glass.
Didn't see.
Sidewalk doesn't splinter,
bird's skull does
when it collides with the thing not seen,
the thing with no give or bend.
Shock absorbed in helmet, skull.
I don't remember falling.
Only pointing left arm, shouting,
"Take Clarke Road, I missed the turn."
Instructions to my daughter pedalling behind me
on a country road, Sunday August morning.

Missed fall, missed rolling.
Missed daughter flagging down a car,
running for help,
holding me until EMTs arrived.
Lost to consciousness
murmuring in a faraway little girl's voice,
"I'm so sorry. I'm so sorry."
Voice of four-year-old who dared
tightrope walk on a low wall,
slipped, fell, broke her arm.
One month without a cast,
not wanting to complain, to be a baby.

Missed pelvis hoisted then like a baby grand
that had been defying gravity, flying music
on pulleys and ropes that snapped
and crashed four flights.
I awoke in traction in the ambulance
my daughter's face above me,
"Mommy, you're going to be all right."
Main block cracked,
certain from avalanche of pain
jackhammers striking marble.
Right to my center,
skullcap to my womb,
armor plate for two pregnancies.
Felled.
Side anvil, blows there too.
Inside tornado tunnel falling
that is vertigo,
holding daughter's hand
for dear life.

UNDRESSING MEN

Even temporary celibacy, I've read,
promises clarity, calm.
Alpine, harpsichord mind.
Feelings pristine, detached.
Then why am I undressing
the Saturn repair associate
or the man who comes to give my garden a bid?
I fumble with buttons,
wanting to run my hand
across flat chest.
The landing field men carry as banners.
My fingertips lingering on nipples,
little clusters of nerves in savannah.
But I can't imagine my kiss there,
or on lips. Not yesterday. Not today.
Not him.

Riding the subway
a man in his twenties, strong jaw,
brushes my arm and I throw him
to the floor. We are alone
on a beach, I open his shirt.
But it's always the same.
I lean ear to chest
unable to detect
heart beating.

AFTER AN UNEXPECTED LATE-NIGHT PHONE CALL WHICH CONCLUDED WITH A POEM READ ALOUD TO ME

One sunflower does not a field in France then make.
One sunflower does not a field in France proclaim.
I am not rounding a bend in Provence
coming upon a glorious throng.
He loves me not.
One sunflower does not a field in France become.
But how I loved
this one.

WHEN ETERNITY BEGINS

In fifth grade, a missionary dressed in white
visited our Stella Maris class.
He asked, "Does anyone know
how long eternity is?"
We did not.
"Imagine a solid iron ball one thousand times
larger than earth floating in space.
Every hundred years, a bird flies by
and as it passes, its wingtip brushes
the sphere. After millions of years,
the iron ball is completely worn away
by the slightest glance of feathers.
Nothing remains.
This is when eternity begins."

I have pondered his story thirty-five years,
imagining the diminishing iron ball,
the bird emerging from darkness,
its silky feather tip brushing the cold, hard sphere
before vanishing into another century.
But it was not until today,
when I missed
your customary quick kiss to my cheek,
that I understood the bird's visit
was nothing for the iron ball to dread.
That gentle brief touch
carrying with it not annihilation,
but eternity.

PRACTICE

Tonight leaning forward
you ask,
"Have you forgiven me yet?"
I answer quickly, "Yes,
have you forgiven me?"
"Yes" you reply gracefully
as Fred Astaire twirls Ginger Rogers.
Not in the movies, but off camera
without top hat or audience.

She wears pedal pushers
and character shoes to practice.
His shirt is open at the collar.
There are missteps, collisions,
exhaustion, laughter.
He places needle mid-record.
Music starts where they left off,
years before they mastered this new routine.

READING TONY HOAGLAND'S POETRY

Dazzled by precision,
I race to his studio
to learn how he mixes that shade of ochre
and the perfect periwinkle blue.
Are the pigments from Lucca?
Is he like my friend Frank,
an artist and plastic surgeon
who says, standing in his studio,
canvasses leaning against walls,
coffee tins of chemicals on his table,
"The paints are slowly
killing me. Toxic fumes
but I gotta have these colors."
On the street below in the meat district,
beef carcasses are hung, then loaded
onto trucks. I wonder how Frank
transports his oversize abstract paintings
and he explains special movers come
who move paintings for a living.
Not every painting meets the public,
but those that do
travel in trucks that could be taken
for moving vans of pianos or watermelons.
"Painting is a lot like surgery,"
he explains, his shoes splattered with paint.
"You give someone the face they think they want,
but make it look like the face they already have
so no one can tell. They just look better. Rested.
And painting is like imagining the face,

making the incision along the ear,
gently tugging flesh back
with precision. Smoothing
lines around eyes, mouth.
Every canvas different.
The man who has his thumb severed at work
wants his thumb back and working
but it means reconstructing his whole hand,
grafting muscle from his shoulder
over to his palm.
He expects a miracle,
the miracle of his thumb back like
the chainsaw never sliced through."
A painting passes by and the man with
his old thumb sewn on passes by
(he holds it to the sunlight, marvels
he can tap his thumb to his forefinger)
and the book of poems
by a master craftsman and artist,
rests on my knees.
His words animated by passion and love,
sharp scalpel in his hand
as he makes the cut to my ear.

SWALLOWING BUTTERFLIES

I swallow butterflies in my sleep.
They dart through jaws ajar,
sweeping passageways
to my heart and lungs.
Colonize there,
cocoons dangling from my ribs.
Precipice of my dreams.

Walking,
lips open, in they fly.
Mouth hoods them.
They depart through my back,
fluttering above shoulder blades
before launch.
New ones take their place,
lifeline before my eyes.
Respirator, deep colors
and pale, shimmery.
I never choke.
It's how I stay alive.

POMEGRANATES

In fifth grade, eighth-grade boys hurled pomegranates
from their play yard across the alley against our classroom
wall.
Thwack, splat, red staining white walls until the next rain
or the janitor hosed juice off. In class, the year went slowly.
In January, my grandfather died.
I was shaken to see my mother cry.
He never cared for me, calling me
and my mother, "Sister."
Gave me a doll the Christmas before
called Pitiful Pearl, laughing as he handed her to me,
"Sister, she reminds me of you."
Designed plain, pug-nosed, patched dress.
I took her into my heart, for who else would?
Then the janitor was killed
crossing the street at dusk
after Mass, a seventeen-year-old girl
leaving Safeway forgot
to turn headlights on.
He had no family so each class
crossed street to mortuary
and prayed. Kneeling, I pondered death.
When my place in line to pass his open casket
came, tears streamed my cheeks.
I knew I was crying for myself, not him,
not my grandfather.
But I couldn't explain this to my seventh-grade sister
who pulled me aside at recess,
scolding me, "Stop embarrassing me.
You don't even know the janitor.

Everyone is talking about you.
Why must you be such a crybaby?"
A question I hadn't the courage to answer.

Then I missed the Iowa Test of Basic Skills,
had to go in on a Saturday alone to make it up.
Wasn't sure what to wear.
Chose flamingo-pink dress with smocking
conscious I dressed more little girl than classmates,
but chubby x dresses offered narrow selection.
I wondered if I was too dressed up,
but I couldn't wear shorts for Sister
or my uniform on a Saturday.
Took my assigned seat in the rear.
Sr. Fidelia read the instructions,
I broke the seal. Began freckling
my bubble sheets with #2 lead smudges.
Then I had to go to the bathroom. Bad.
Through vocabulary then arithmetic. I could hold it.
I couldn't raise my hand during the test
and ask to be excused. She'd want
to know why and I'd have to say
bathroom aloud.
After fractions, I finally raised my hand,
but she was bent over her desk.
I would have to shout out.

"Time's up for section 2. Put your pencil down."
I prayed she'd read my mind
and she did, suggesting I take fresh air.
I slipped out my bowels churning,
down the hall to the girls' bathroom.
Locked. Locked!

I tried the boy's door. Locked.
I slinked back to my classroom.

"Are you ready for section 3?"
she asked, smiling.
I took my seat. "Reading comprehension."
The avalanche began. I couldn't hold it back.
I was shitting in my pants
but I didn't use those words because
my mother taught us scientific terms
so we wouldn't be ashamed of our bodies.
Bowel movements. BM. I was perched atop
my own excrement — from the Latin —.
Section 3 required great concentration.
I dove like a pelican with saddlebags.
Thank God she was sitting in the front.
I prayed she couldn't smell me.

When I finished the test,
I was careful not to run from the room,
drawing suspicion or losing my smashed cargo.
I backed out the door, thanking her,
and ran to the alley where my father
was waiting to drive me home.
I burst into tears.
"Hard test?" he asked.
I shook my head, sobbing.
"That smell?" he probed.
"The bathroom door was locked," I choked.

Looking out the car window, I saw two boys
throwing pomegranates, come to play on a Saturday.
I realized I had never seen them throw,
just heard from inside class.

Boys in my grade knew better than to touch
what belonged to older ones.
My father turned on the car.
I wanted to hurl a pomegranate
and watch it smash open and I
wanted to protect every pomegranate
from their stupid, cruel, pointless game.
I wanted to take one home, like a just hatched duckling.
We pulled out of the alley.

"When we get home,
take a bath. You'll feel a lot better,"
my father casually remarked.
"No one needs to know."

In a family of six nosy, teasing children,
where privacy was scarce,
if my mother or siblings ever knew,
they never said a word to me.
Nor did he.

It happened but he made it so it also never happened.
Or it didn't matter that it happened.
I paid no price.
Years later, when he left us,
it was times like the drive home in my pink dress
after the Iowa test,
that made letting him go feel like
I was standing behind school holding pomegranates.
Being in the fifth grade, and a girl,
my job to save them.

MEG CAMPBELL grew up with five siblings in La Jolla, California, where she attended parochial and public schools and the Bishop's School for Girls. After graduating from Radcliffe College, she worked as a community organizer in Arkansas, Texas, Louisiana, and Vermont; legislative research director at the Massachusetts State Senate; and teacher and administrator in the Boston and Chelsea Public Schools.

Currently a Lecturer at the Harvard Graduate School of Education and Executive Director of Expeditionary Learning Outward Bound, she holds an M.S. from Wheelock College and a C.A.S. from Harvard Graduate School of Education. She teaches a poetry immersion course for teachers at Teachers and Writers Collaborative in New York City.

Meg Campbell is presently working with William Duke on an anthology of poems about divorce, *Split Verse: Poems to Heal the Heart*, and with her daughters on a collection of poetry and prose celebrating menarche, *Flying Off the Roof.* Her daughters Moriah, a senior at Wellesley College, and Adrienne, a sophomore at Barnard College, call Boston their home.

LINDA BASTIAN regards the flower as a powerful metaphor for life: delicate, complex, self-renewing, compelling, various in its colors and forms.

She grew up in New England and has been exhibiting her work in museums and galleries since 1970. Although formally trained during the Abstract Expressionism period, her interest in nature and the mystery of beautiful and sensuous ideas and forms, is the central theme in her work of birds, fish, animals, and flowers.

She holds a Ph.D. in Art Education from New York University and was long-time chairperson of the Art Education Department at the School of Visual Arts in New York City.

Her work is in the collections of major corporations and has been included in numerous museum group and solo shows around the country.

She currently lives in upstate New York.

ILLUSTRATIONS

PHOTO CREDITS

Cover photograph courtesy of
Photographic Archives, Vanderbilt University

Typographic Design: Barbara Bergeron
Cover Design: MOG

MEG CAMPBELL

MIDMARCH ARTS BOOKS

Documenting Women in the Arts

Gumbo Ya Ya: Anthology of Contemporary African-American Women Artists

Women Artists of Italian Futurism — Almost Lost to History

Expanding Circles: Women, Art & Community

Camera Fiends and Kodak Girls II: 60 Selections By and About
Women in Photography 1855-1965

Camera Fiends and Kodak Girls I: 50 Selections By and About
Women in Photography 1840-1930

The Heart of the Question: Writings & Paintings of Howardena Pindell

Michelangelo and Me: Six Years in My Italian Haven

The Lady Architects: Lois Lilley Howe, Eleanor Manning,
and Mary Almy, 1893-1937

Modernism & Beyond: Women Artists of the Pacific Northwest

Yesterday and Tomorrow: California Women Artists

No Bluebonnets, No Yellow Roses: Texas Women in the Arts

Pilgrims and Pioneers: New England Women in the Arts

Women Artists of the World

American Women Artists: Works on Paper

When Even the Cows Were Up: Drawings & Stories of an
Artist's Life Spanning the 20th century

— History —

Art and Politics in the 1930s: Modernism, Marxism, and Americanism

Tarnished Silver: After the Photo Boom,
Essays on Photography 1979-1989

Beyond Walls and Wars: Art, Politics, and Multiculturalism

Mutiny and the Mainstream: Talk That Changed Art, 1975-1990

— Poetry and Images—

Solo Crossing

Sight Lines

Whirling Round the Sun

Parallels: 3 Artists/ 47 Women Poets

Illuminations: Images for "Asphodel, That Greeny Flower"

Images From Dante

Voices of Women: 3 critics on 3 poets on 3 artists/heroines

— Creatures —

Artists and Their Cats

The Little Cat Who Had No Name

— Information —

Artists Colonies, Retreats & Study Centers

Whole Arts Directory

Guide to Women's Art Organizations and Directory for the Arts